HAL•LEONARD

VIOLIN PLAY-ALONG

HOT JAZZ

CONTENTS

Page	Title	Demo Track	Play-Along Track
2	Body and Soul	1	2
4	Dark Eyes	3	4
7	The Hot Canary	5	6
10	How High the Moon	7	8
13	My Blue Heaven	9	10
16	Summertime	11	12
19	Sweet Georgia Brown	13	14
22	This Can't Be Love	15	16
	TUNING NOTES	17	

ISBN 978-1-4768-7543-9

HAL•LEONARD®
CORPORATION
7777 W. BLUEMOUND RD. P.O. BOX 13819 MILWAUKEE, WI 53213

Jon Vriesacker, Violin
Tom McGirr, Bass
Kirk Tatnall, Guitar
Dan Maske, Piano, Percussion

Audio Arrangements by Dan Maske

Visit Hal Leonard Online at
www.halleonard.com

Body and Soul

Words by Edward Heyman, Robert Sour and Frank Eyton
Music by John Green

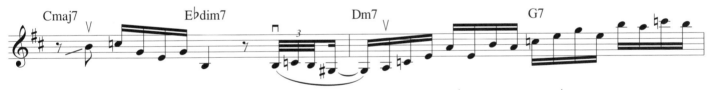

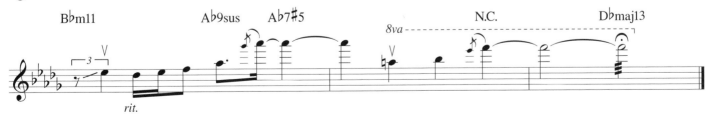

Dark Eyes

Words and Music by Bob Dylan

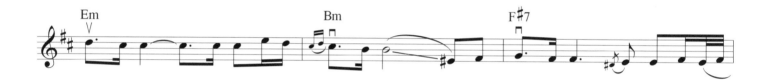

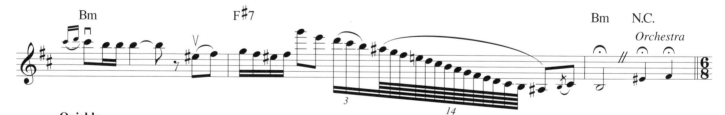

Bright Swing

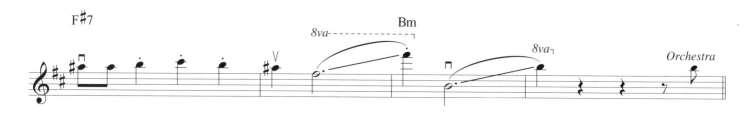

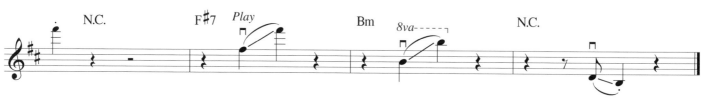

The Hot Canary

Music by Paul Nero

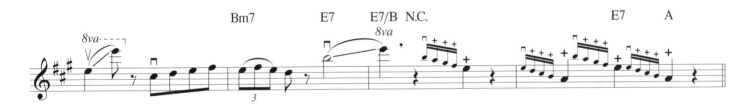

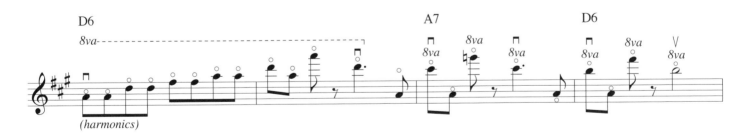

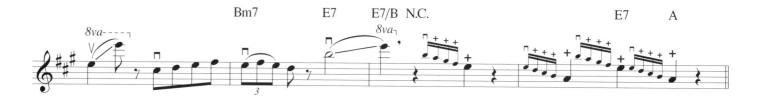

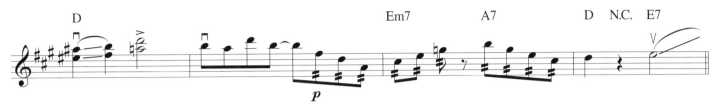

Very Fast

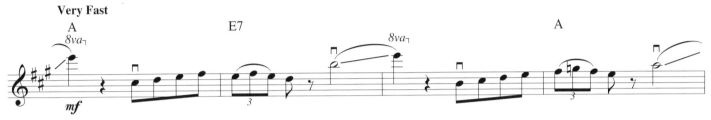

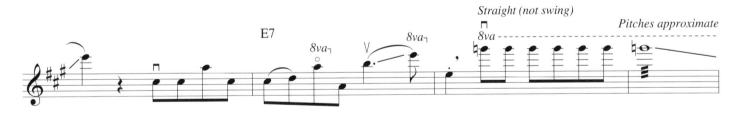

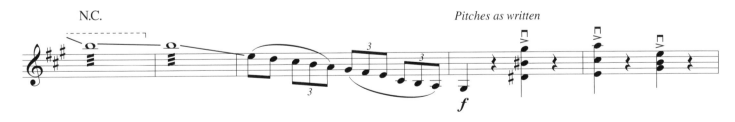

How High the Moon

from TWO FOR THE SHOW

Lyrics by Nancy Hamilton
Music by Morgan Lewis

Bright Swing

Guitar doubles violin 8vb

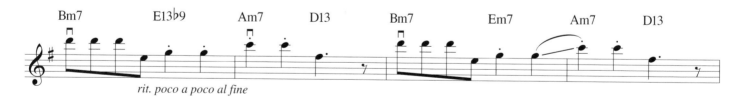

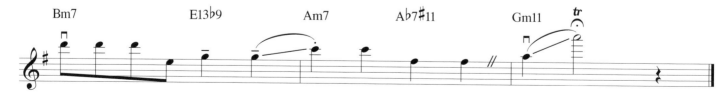

My Blue Heaven

Lyric by George Whiting
Music by Walter Donaldson

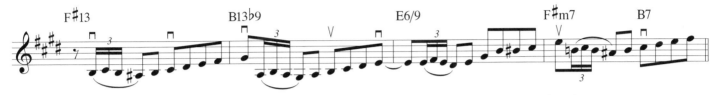

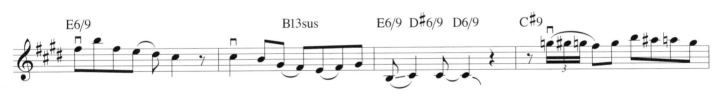

Summertime

from PORGY AND BESS®

Music and Lyrics by George Gershwin, DuBose and Dorothy Heyward and Ira Gershwin

Bright Swing (subito)

17

Much Slower (straight eighths)

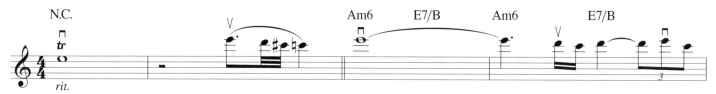

Slowly, Freely

Sweet Georgia Brown

Words and Music by Ben Bernie, Maceo Pinkard and Kenneth Casey

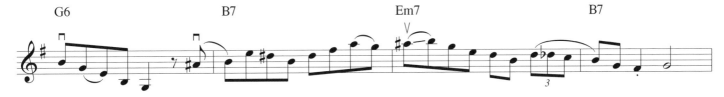

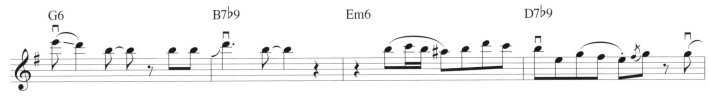

This Can't Be Love

from THE BOYS FROM SYRACUSE

Words by Lorenz Hart
Music by Richard Rodgers

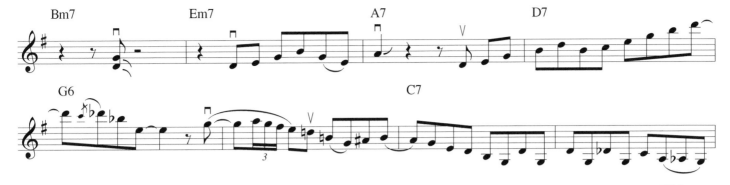